Through the Looking Glass

Through the Looking Glass

Poems

ANNA CATES

RESOURCE *Publications* • Eugene, Oregon

THROUGH THE LOOKING GLASS
Poems

Copyright © 2026 Anna Cates. All rights reserved. Except for brief quotations in critical publications or reviews, no part of this book may be reproduced in any manner without prior written permission from the publisher. Write: Permissions, Wipf and Stock Publishers, 199 W. 8th Ave., Suite 3, Eugene, OR 97401.

Resource Publications
An Imprint of Wipf and Stock Publishers
199 W. 8th Ave., Suite 3
Eugene, OR 97401

www.wipfandstock.com

PAPERBACK ISBN: 979-8-3852-6366-0
HARDCOVER ISBN: 979-8-3852-6367-7
EBOOK ISBN: 979-8-3852-6368-4

VERSION NUMBER 011326

For Fifi and "Tom Cat"

For now we see through a glass, darkly; but then face to face.

—1 Corinthians 13:12

Contents

Acknowledgments | ix
Introduction | xi

One
Through the Looking Glass | 2
Fork in the Woods | 3
The Red Queen | 4
Broken Pieces | 5
The White Rabbit | 7
Miracle on Elm Street | 8
Cod Liver Oil Discovery | 9
The Cheshire Cat | 10
The White Queen | 11
In Retrospect | 12
Alice | 14

Two
Folk Tales | 16
Magic Mirror | 17
Shield Maiden | 18
Twin Worlds | 19
The Queen | 20
Poison Apple | 21
A Gothic Shade of Pale | 22

It Wasn't as If . . . | 23
Charming | 24
Witching | 25
Misty Meadows | 26
Magic Mirror: The Account | 27
The Looking Glass: An Afterwards | 28
The Blood | 29
when at last we let the light | 31

Three
Unnatural | 34
Count Orlock | 35
Omens | 36
A Hunger, Nearly Quenched | 37
NPD | 38
Vampire: A Found Poem | 39
Porphyria's Lover | 40
Case No. 4758 | 42
Model V666 | 43

Four
Bride of Frankenstein | 46
The Frog Child | 47
Goblin Spree | 48
Strange Worlds | 49
At the Ruins of Sarpedon | 50
Crocodile Tears Trickle Down | 51
a wave shifts . . . | 53
Terraforming Mars | 54
Epoceclipse Word Find | 55

Acknowledgments

Many thanks to the following publications and organizations that recognized and/or published poems in this collection, some with minor edits or different titles, and some newly combined with other poems:

One:

Bones: "cool dawn . . ." (added to "Through the Looking Glass")
Cattails: "Broken Pieces"
Contemporary Haibun Online: "The Red Queen"
Drifting Sands: "Fork in the Woods"
Electric Cat City: A Poesy (Red Moon Press, 2023): "The Cheshire Cat," "Cod Liver Oil Discovery," "Miracle on Elm Street," "Alice"
Little Black Box: Speculative Poetry from Ohio (Resource Publications, 2023): "Alice"
The Other Bunny: "In Retrospect," "The White Rabbit"
Voice of Eve: "Through the Looking Glass"

2022 Rhysling Award nominee: "Alice"
2023 Ohio Poetry Day *Better Late than Never Contest*: "The Red Queen," Honorable Mention

Two:

Cattails: "wild roses" (originally titled "Meditations of Infinity," added to "Charming")
Disabled Tales: "The Looking Glass: An Afterwards," "Magic Mirror: The Account"

Acknowledgments

Dwarf Stars 2025 (SFPA, 2025): "It Wasn't as If," "cobblestone trail" (added to "It Wasn't as If"), "the path away" (added to "Shield Maiden")
Scarlet Dragonfly: "Witching"
*Star*Line*: "Twin Worlds"
Voice of Eve: "Shield Maiden"

2022 SFPA Poetry Contest, Dwarf Form Category: "It Wasn't as If," Honorable Mention
2023 SFPA Poetry Contest, Short Poem Category: "Charming," Honorable Mention

Three:

The 2025 Rhysling Anthology (SFPA, 2025): "Porphyria's Lover"
Contemporary Haibun Online: "Vampire: A Found Poem"
Disabled Tales: haiku portion of "Unnatural" and "Count Orlock"
Drifting Sands: "A Hunger, Nearly Quenched"
Electric Cat City: A Poesy (Red Moon Press, 2023): "NPD"
SFPA 2024 Valentine's Day Poetry Reading: "A Hunger, Nearly Quenched"

Four:

Abyss & Apex: "At the Ruins of Sarpedon"
*Star*Line*: "a wave shifts . . ."

Introduction

The following is a collection of mostly previously published speculative short-form poems. Each piece is intended to be read as one of the following forms: haibun, tanka prose, tanka, tanka sequence, or haiku sequence—though some are experimental. Several works have been revised from their original versions or combined with others to create what I hope is a cohesive collection, unified both by form and by the motif of the mirror.

One

What is essential is invisible to the eye.
—Antoine de Saint-Exupéry, *The Little Prince*

THROUGH THE LOOKING GLASS

"But I don't want to go among mad people," Alice remarked. "Oh, you can't help that," said the Cat: "we're all mad here."
—Lewis Carroll, *Alice's Adventures in Wonderland*

Alice peers through the looking glass
(a queen of hearts in a kingdom of voyeurs)
at cotton candy clouds, moving westward
so montivagant. Shady characters slump
beneath shady trees above the gloomy flume.
Worms smoke dope on magic mushrooms,
and the Jabberwocky *vrooms* across
the vestiges of violaceous charisma
blushing each sunrise to sunset
warm pinkish secrets.

She is no coward struck with
catoptrophobia. Yet now is not the time
for fanfaronade to gorgonize the cavalcade
bound to the Red Queen's ktenology,
for here no anarchist antidotes loom.
She must flee her own hamartia
while her house of cards yet stands,
while cats yet grin and rabbits run,
while pigs have wings and dodos roam,
she can still go home.

    cool dawn the rabbit tastes the dew tastes the rabbit

FORK IN THE WOODS

The moon shimmers
Like a magic looking glass
Thin as ice
Or fat as a red delicious
Alice pauses
Only for a moment
As the Cheshire Cat's eyes grow
Larger than the Big Bad Wolf's
Kaleidoscopes of color swirl
Crazier than the cosmos
Deeper than a black hole
But this is her story
In woods duskier than forgetfulness
She remembers her sister
Reading to her beneath the oak
She chooses which road to take
And walks on . . .

    "O," "R," "U"
    a difficult question
    in smoke rings

THE RED QUEEN

halo of the moon
one nonplussed puss that Cheshire Cat
but this time *you* are Alice
that insufferable dodo bird
you must choose your own adventure
but what kind of choice is *that*, you wonder
fists clenched, beholding a dark path
compounded with thunder and lightning
and you wonder more and more
for this *is* wonderland, not to be confused
with wonderful, and not to suggest
you don't feel confused
for everything confounds you
clouds you like smoke rings
till you wax motion sick
tossed by ocean waves
not in a boat but as a castaway
a throwaway who's lost her flotsam
you hop on top a Mock Turtle
for it's the only ride and the hour is late
you sail closer, closer, closer
to a dark and nebulous fate

    rustling sea oats
    mother of pearl horizon
    tide's end
    the inroads and inlands
    inside of us

BROKEN PIECES

I am not crazy; my reality is just different from yours.
—Cheshire Cat[1]

long winter
on old psychiatric records
Rorschach coffee stain

    Getting approved for foster parenting becomes more involved than I'd anticipated. Family Services suggests I undertake a complete psychological evaluation . . .
    I muddle over six hundred questions, some I'm unsure how to answer. T/F: *I'm never happier than when I'm alone.* A repeated question. *True* could mean totally antisocial or simply equally content in group or solo. Reluctantly, I select *True*. Probably, I should have left it blank.
    On to the interview. "Do you have demons?" the psychologist asks, sitting across from me behind her desk.
    "No, they stay away from me," I reply, fingering the crucifix at my throat, taking the question quite literally . . .
    "What does this statement mean to you: *Blood is thicker than water?*"
    "*Blood* is a figurative expression for kinship. It means *family first.*"
    She nods her head. "And what does this statement mean: *People in glass houses shouldn't throw stones?*"
    "It means you shouldn't say of others what they could say of you." Weird coincidence that, only days prior to the evaluation,

---

1. Misattributed.

that rhetorical expression was utilized in a parenting book in an explanation of adolescent cognitive progression from concrete to figurative thinking. Otherwise, I'd never have known!

Before the day ends, I emphasize that it's been well over twenty years since I've experienced any psychiatric problems.

Weeks later, I'm mailed a diagnosis: Schizoid Personality Disorder... So much for foster parenting...

Mad Hatter's Tea Party
scent of cinnamon rolls
and wet mouse

THE WHITE RABBIT

Straight down the rabbit hole—
Never a *goodbye*, never a *hello*—
He is more nonsensical
Than you know,
Always in a hurry
To get nowhere fast,
Like the driver who'll pass you,
So impatient, on the road
When you're already speeding.
But he is late, late,
For a very important date—
Will call Mary Ann "Alice"
And Alice "Mary Ann."
And what's up with that?
Who is his dream girl anyway,
And does *he* even know?

> a fat bee lands
> on a lazy daisy . . .
> the riverbank

MIRACLE ON ELM STREET

Raise the dead.

—Matthew 10:8

One month from my fifty-first birthday, in the first warm flush of spring, I take a neighborhood stroll, the top clasps of my polka-dot shirt unfastened to admit the mellow breeze.

"You have a wonderful evening, ma'am!" A lorry driver grins at me like the Cheshire Cat, leaning out the window of his truck and sopping up the verdant air. Ghost-like, he tips his invisible hat then vanishes down the lane.

Half amused, half alarmed, I refasten the top clasp of my shirt and turn for home.

> magpie melody
> mystifying me . . .
> March meltdown

COD LIVER OIL DISCOVERY

A land was full of wonder, mystery, and danger. Some say, to survive it, you need to be as mad as a hatter. Which, luckily, I am.

—Mad Hatter, *Alice in Wonderland*[2]

As Victorian England scuttles into the Industrial Age, orphans, residing in sewers, lick discarded fish scraps off the walls and develop a noticeable resistance to rickets . . .

bare feet
covered in soot
fuliginous skies

uliginous passages
in a shadowy corner
rat catcher's hitch

---

2. The 2010 film.

THE CHESHIRE CAT

"I don't like the looks of it," said the King: "however, it may kiss my hand, if it likes."
"I'd rather not," the Cat remarked.
—Lewis Carroll, *Alice's Adventures in Wonderland*

Some say, *you have to play your cards right*, others, *the cards you're dealt determine all*. Some see a descending order, chain of being: King, Queen, Jack, Joker, wild, the rest, the masses, just numbers, numbers, statistics.

"I'm a statistic now," I've said before about doleful this or that, getting cancer or whatnot. But on brighter days I even imagine within the cards some wonderland.

Clubs, spades, diamonds, hearts—they bear their own symbolism—the Queen of Hearts cliché. Some simply see the innate fragility inherent in a house of cards. No matter how full—how sad—it always topples in the end.

belly of the tank—
two soldiers and a demon
playing Durak*

*a traditional Russian card game

THE WHITE QUEEN

Why, sometimes I've believed as many as six impossible things before breakfast.

—Lewis Carroll, *Through the Looking-Glass*

We could spend our whole lives painting the roses red, though our dimensions pale to thin as cards. But true enough, all is not as it seems. Fake flowers are made for gravestones.

    a false god,
    eyes doped,
    worming up . . .
    smoke ring halo

IN RETROSPECT

"I weep for you," the Walrus said.
"I deeply sympathize."
—Lewis Carroll, *Through the Looking-Glass*

Alice, life is a curious madhouse.
People shuffle in and out.
Somebody wants your head.
Every path leads to somewhere,
but you can't go back to yesterday.

Never disappear for good.
But if you do
crawl through the wrong door,
come to the wrong party,
break your teacup—
eat me, drink me
such beautiful soup—
lose your muchness till you don't
care which way you ought to go,
tomorrow is always another day
to while away and naysay,

tweedle by the sea
till your torso turns to paper,
you drip sand like an hourglass,
or your pig with wings flies in
to take you away, and you wake
from nonsense or reason.

day moon
a strange elixir
morning dreams

ALICE

She longed to live in that magical world where the white rabbit roamed, to peer in the wishing well, wafting its cool draft, to know that wishes can come true. But the old folks, misunderstanding her "silly dreams," scoffed at her ideas, telling her to think more "sensible thoughts." At that, she wept.

Yet dreams are magic to those who truly believe. She planted a tree from the magical seeds of her mind, and it grew. Rising and billowing, it grew, erupting with seeds of its own. Wind scattered the seeds, near and far.

She also grew, with her garden, then her forest, into a woman—and there thrived many a wild thing. Yet it was never too cold or damp, and fireflies played their part, making the darkness bright.

Long after the old woman died, legends spoke of a cobblestone well, mossy and crumbly, deep within the forest, and a voice that haunted those miles.

"Come child," she calls, her voice young again, like the apple trees that bloom anew each spring. "Come to my well. Come dream with me."

>   prayer stone
>   warmed by her hand
>   sound of water . . .

Two

And though my eyes were open
They might just as well've been closed.

—Procol Harum, *A Whiter Shade of Pale*

FOLK TALES

beyond the heath
and woodland border
a hidden trail winds
down to the cottage
of the seven dwarfs

a thatched roof
and cobble chimney—
propped in a corner
a broom, but where
is mistress ma'am?

prophecies end
though legends remain
effervescent wind
sparkles enchantment
on sporadic eventides

MAGIC MIRROR

Kaleidoscopic shards color souls into flowers, into stars, ripple like warped time, riddle like the wizened.

To some, the glass is dark, cold dimness that never shines like brass, shows only statues, kings and queens no more than monsters.

    flipped images
    make mischief or amends
    in a parallel world
    myriad sounds and hues
    Milky Way

SHIELD MAIDEN

some girls wait
in a castle
others call
a cage

they wait
for the red cape
to come flashing
a prince with perfect teeth
and polished boots

they wait
for their gardens to grow
they say it takes
a lot of rain

alone in their bower
they watch
the parade pass by
they dream
of roses that never fade

in a world full of princes
full of monsters too

> the path away
> from the self
> leading to
> the self . . .
> an imposing castle

TWIN WORLDS

Two kingdoms poised in parallel: In one, waterfalls cascaded down, in the other, splashed up with flying fish, wings and flanks bursting into dragons, raging fire. But in the other kingdom, flames froze. One tower rose; the other sank into an underground labyrinth. Alone in her bower, she gazed into her magic mirror, beauty mark on the wrong lip, oil painting topsy-turvy, candelabra on the wrong side, and she swooned, unable to glean which paramour spoke true when promising castles, positing bliss, coiling around her with a lingering hiss, killing her with a shattering kiss.

fractured culture—
polarized factions threatened
with meltdown . . .

Long nails
and a pouty smirk:
"Bring me her heart!"

THE QUEEN

silk the darkest red to sheen of black—
horn headdress fluttering gray gossamer—
she glowers at the simple peasant
in patched leather. "I'll have her heart!"
She licks her lips, a dark angel, a Circe,
soiled by subterfuge and spell craft
that have streaked the chamber walls black.
Murder a noble child and rightful heir?
How can he dare?
"Bring me her heart, or would you rather?"
She gestures toward the oubliette.
He shudders at the bottle dungeon.
The tension grows heavier than darkness.
He sinks to his knees.
"Your will is mine, Milady!"

    old castle
    through cracked mortar
    a shadow, weeping

POISON APPLE

what pleases the eye
may deceive an Eve—
forbidden flesh

she bites then bows
before the glass, thirsty,
yet cannot drink

drifting, yet frozen,
gazing, yet unseeing—
the blind blood moon

vampire—
are you now a god,
will you live forever,

commune, undead,
partake of sacred bread,
manna from Heaven?

A GOTHIC SHADE OF PALE

Just one bite it didn't matter how big
or small that chunk of juicy snow-white
flesh surrounded by so crisp and sweet
crimson as Eve's sin sister act succulent
enough to turn you succubus but no
she cannot she cannot she can hardly
breath just that one piece spinning visions
as Rumpelstiltskin's loom spiraling
fate askew as a scorned fairy's hex hissing
puddling a gothic princess on the grass

    day moon fading
    the pink blossoms
    of her cheeks

IT WASN'T AS IF . . .

stone gargoyles would leap off cathedrals and accost her,
simple pedestrians would morph into urban werewolf
and swallow her whole,
golden wheels whirling inside her inner eye
would clash with a nebulous crescent,
pink flowers plucked in the wilds
would poison and define the skull cradled in her arms
while melancholy piano notes sifted through shadowy woods
and fire angels cried while little dragons flittered through her soul
like butterflies and waters deluged red Mars,
turning to fecund green atomic desolation—
starlight could never stop glistening in those eyes,
that she could close her eyes, close her eyes, forever, forever!

    cobblestone trail
    leading to the sunset—
    fire angles . . .
    stone after stone
    how can hearts be healed?

CHARMING

she dreams she is lost
in a black and white forest
arrives at a red, red rose
the scent impossibly sweet

cold and colorless skies crystallize
a glass ceiling she cannot break
imprisoned by that bitter bite
of red delicious, forever
stuck in her throat

she dreams the sky rises
warm lips press against hers
barriers lift like a dispelled hex
she awakens to his strangeness
no worn leather but emerald velvet
tall and svelte and narrow of nose
so unlike the little folk

she does not fall madly in love
but takes his perfumed hand—
wrist rimmed with lace,
finger embossed with a gem—
accepts his help, accepts her fate
to vindicate her family name
and save her people

> wild roses
> will not outlast your lips
> will not outlast
> the truth they tell
> could last forever . . .

WITCHING

    Her arrival at the village changes everything. Fallen leaves rise into human form, then march forward.
    Like wolves or rabbits, she attracts her own share of huntsmen, yet remains elusive.

cloven tracks
flood with rainwater—
a blackbird's thin *seeeeee*

raw deer heart
fouler than fair
the weather

MISTY MEADOWS

Courtly gossip led me to believe
a wolf had devoured Snow,
the castoff princess, sole heir
of the grand and glorious White Dynasty!
Then Red tells me she's taken the hand
of some foppish buffoon named *Charming*.
Oh, how she rose from the gutter,
aroused such rumors, returning to pomp!

At the banquet to celebrate Snow's wedding,
waiting on tables, I watched in slack-jawed horror
as her in-laws made the fallen queen wear
those red-hot iron shoes! I'll never forget
her mother-in-law cackling, "Dance for us!
You lovely pixie, dance!" And that broken beast,
feet smoking, slumped outside, leaving
behind a blood trail like a slug.

Nobles are crooked as haunted trees.
A pox on them! Don't breathe a word,
but I hope they all fade away, drift into legend,
into myth, dissolve like dew into the mist!

> fragrant garland
> adorning the unicorn
> summer's fancy

MAGIC MIRROR: THE ACCOUNT

The poisoned apple was her idea.
She shunned her angel side and hooked up
with a demon, loitered in the cellar,
dungeoned like the doomed, whirled up
frothy potions, casting spells that stained
her dainty fingers black and blue.
Yet Snow White returned with a prince!

After that, nothing I said could appease her.
She tried to break me, hurling a wine goblet
at her reflection. But when that failed—
for magic mirrors never break just as true
as magic mirrors never lie—she threatened
to throw herself from the balcony. I summoned
a premonition into view: her body, warped
and twisted in the weeds, devoured by death
like Jezebel's dogs. "What end could be worse
than that?" she snapped and slammed shut
the door of her bower.

>   a lover
>   all in green—
>   the hounds
>   smiling

THE LOOKING GLASS: AN AFTERWARDS

Beauty is a simple passion,
but, oh my friends, in the end . . .

—Anne Sexton, "Snow White and the Seven Dwarfs"

    Do not doubt me. Magic mirrors never lie. And do not try to break me. Magic mirrors never crack. But you will reap the seven years bad luck just the same.
    Controversial though I am, most of what you see in me is just your own reflection. Yet you are more transparent than you think, albeit rippled. Indeed, I am no omniscient god. On some days, cloudy skies shed no color on the waters. And some pools are murky, bogs heaven-laden with frogs . . .
    In the end, I could barely discern her, the troubled queen, hidden behind her demon, Arabesque.
    Lightning strikes where it will. I am but an interpreter of shadows.

better a mile
in ruby slippers . . .
red-hot iron shoes

THE BLOOD

I

Inside her weakness, darkly framed,
three drops of blood fell on an ivory
canvas. She saw beauty in the stain,
spoke, more prophecy than wish, of legacy
in contrasts both grim and good.

Before the breaking, there is blood.
Before the water bursts, first pains attack.
From open caves, rivers gush, never come back.
Redbirds rush in a frenzy, along the riverbank,
a dust of snow, a huntsman all in black.

Sacramental water, wine, and bread—
a child is born, a mother dead.

II

Though frost may ice a cold-bloomed rose
and night shroud them both,
love endures the cruelest season, bestows
the warmth to waken seeds.

How bright even a winter sun.
That warmth clears the mist,
dispels any lingering gloom, our ruin,
sanctifies maiden and prince.

Petals, or a rubied Judas' kiss?
The Blood redeems the sin-oppressed,
corrupted flesh, burns ice deep as ebony.
That fire dances on the snow!

    a weeping angel
    has no color . . .
    River of Heaven
    still waters reflect
    infinity's depth

WHEN AT LAST WE LET THE LIGHT

warm our lids
and open the eyes
of our heart
we'll no longer seek
magic mirrors
or scrying stones
and will at last
see clearly

> on a quiet lake
> the moon's reflection . . .
> scent of roses

Three

Taking up the shaving glass, I looked in it. As I did so, I could not suppress a start, for not only was he close to me, but I could see him over my shoulder. But there was no reflection of him in the mirror! The whole room behind me was displayed; but there was no sign of a man in it, except myself.

—Bram Stoker, *Dracula*

UNNATURAL

a vampire's face
through the looking glass
betrays no reflection—
living in shadow . . .
beyond moral judgement?

old memories
growing cobwebs
squeak of a bat

COUNT ORLOCK

blood
his soul's opiate—
wolfsbane moon

forbidden thirst—
a friend's injury
just eye candy

reflectionless "other"
unforgivable shadow
Nosferatu

     twilight . . .
     the melancholy color
     of complicity

OMENS

a spider
eyeing a bat
eyeing your neck . . .

Transylvania—What flowers there bloom? What beauty, what doom? Beneath Carpathian peaks, beneath a portending wolf moon?

pale feet
silent as starlight . . .
the long wind

A HUNGER, NEARLY QUENCHED

He was the vampire
drinking the fire
of red peonies
flooding Romanian hills . . .
He was the fantasist
frolicking in effulgent lilac
baptized among water lilies
purified by snowy daffodil
pining the beautiful
narcissus

dusk
we nearly touch
stardust

NPD

Narcissus worshiped it, his own reflection in the stream. But oh, the pain those ripples wrought!

One cannot truly own oneself. To want is not to have, neither is to see—the world dangling on a string. We try to master it. We reach and reach, yet it is always just out of grasp!

human
shadows
shifting
skyscrapers
personality
disorder

VAMPIRE: A FOUND POEM

Psychics can see the color of time it's blue.
The past is a foreign country; they do things differently there.
Ships at a distance have every man's wish on board.
Where now? Who now? When now?
In the beginning, sometimes I left messages in the street.
I am a sick man . . . I am a spiteful man.
In a sense, I am Jacob Horner.
He was born with a gift of laughter and a sense that the world was mad.

> *no lips*
> *left to howl*
> *yet dreams*
> *of cedar and sage*
> *a gentle twilight*

Lines (first lines from each book) taken in order from:
Ronald Sukenick, *Blown Away*, L. P. Hartley, *The Go-Between*, Zora Neale Hurston, *Their Eyes Were Watching God*, Samuel Beckett, *The Unnamable*, David Markson, *Wittgenstein's Mistress*, Fyodor Dostoyevsky, *Notes from Underground*, John Barth, *The End of the Road*, Raphael Sabatini, *Scaramouche*.

PORPHYRIA'S LOVER

She is his summer fruit
and autumn harvest—
He tastes in her
the change
in seasons
spring grass
in cow's milk
first dandelions
in her blood
even the moon
full and mesmerizing
on thawing
lake water

When the green deepens
buzzes to life
with honeybees
he hears them
through diurnal dreams
droning throughout
the countryside
terrible and bright
far beyond his casket
his soul as riddled
with holes as a hive

In his nightmare
he dons a top hat
and stylish walking stick
picnics with her
in a meadow

of daffodils
laughs merrily
like a dandy—
They devour
fresh strawberries
and cream
rich fecundity
dripping from
their chins . . .

He awakens
screaming in agony
gagging on his tongue—
Oh, what hope remains
for the damned?
He can never behold
a field of wildflowers—
His eyes open
only in the dark

    the pulse
    about her neck—
    night rose

CASE NO. 4758

Everyone loves to stick it to an evil fiend . . .
But first we must hear from his lawyer:

He has no possibility of peace.
His sleep is dreamless surcease.
His coffin is no sepulcher for saints.
He is lifeless as a gargoyle.
His eyes shine like diamonds in fear of your stake.
You terrorize with your cross.
You think you're brave to kill with your bare hands
his castle's fat black spiders?
You imagine him with leathery wings, flapping
off to a full-bodied moon, his dark hair wild
with wicked wind. You could never fathom
his vocabulary for night, but did you ever consider
his sickening beauty? Did you ever love him?

    Endless confinement\upside down\starlight

MODEL V666

from a drone's height, a *service-them*
aims at sentient life the size of ants,
slogging through the swamps and on
to piles of sawdust, once a great forest.
and once where honeybees thrived
a dead breeze buzzes radioactive particles.
the new model promises mass destruction,
reads minds, smells and catalogues sweat,
interprets and records whispers, soft as ear hairs,
contains programmed memories of blood's
irony taste, and the claim is, even an urge for it,
or maybe that was just deceptive advertising,
to dub the model, *the vampire* . . .

> cosmonaut
> with the crumbling mouth—
> radioactive stew

What if everyone in the galaxy forgot their rage
and voiced instead of angst this simple plea:
To all I've ever wronged, please forgive me . . .

Four

The eyes of a stranger are mirrors to our own selves.
—Anonymous proverb

BRIDE OF FRANKENSTEIN

such witchy science—
her skunk-striped hair sizzles
with electric charge

burnt chemical scent—
her lips the tint
of dried blood

her eyes pop
in the looking glass—
scars and bandages

a monster's
perfect mate—
how old wounds ache

THE FROG CHILD

crab grass whiskers
and voice wispy
as a wasp—
a fiery fiddlestick
that Rumpelstiltskin!

yet who can tell
wild man from wizard
from twisted mandrake—
Rumpelstiltskin . . .
gaze into the mirror,

child, and tell me why
you tarried in the loathsome
wilds—oh, why did you
venture where you knew
you ought not go?

GOBLIN SPREE

Thugla, the goblin, strolled into Troll Town.
Her ragged gaze roved over tacky knick-knacks.
Gaga for clutter, she gobbled it down.
Thugla, the goblin, went to town!
She haggled and crooned in handsomest frown
each peddler as rods and whips crick cracked.
Thugla, the goblin, tramped through town,
her ragged gaze crazed with knick-knacks.

    smoggy sunset
    in a squalid handbag
    vanity mirror

STRANGE WORLDS

Miracle and mirror have the same root. It is a very ancient root. It is the word for "to look" or "to see."

—Peter S. Beagle, *The Last Unicorn*

        hiding in nori
        a scraggly-haired mermaid . . .
        sea lice

Like Oedipus Rex, an old King Lear, a cur, despised and betrayed through his daughters' filial ingratitude, lapped at his wounds with the one consolation: becoming blind, he could finally see.

        purple brain coral
        a seahorse coursing
        dappled sunlight

At his castle by the sea, a young Prince Lear couldn't glean the magic. Blindly devoted, he did not realize his beloved, Lady Amalthea, was really a unicorn!

        a horse's lips
        frothy as the sea
        first stars

AT THE RUINS OF SARPEDON

*Perseus**

son of a god
his magic bag shimmers
ocean's edge

man of flesh
light in winged sandals
world's end

fright and horror
in a frozen gaze
helm of darkness

dizzying rattling
a stricken warrior's
marble pose

snake heads
ooze pink oil
he slips forward

polished shield mirror
he swerves his sword
and severs the head

*And he, looking not at her directly, but viewing her in the reflection of the bronze shield which he bore, cut off her head.

—Apollodorus, *Bibliotheca*

CROCODILE TEARS TRICKLE DOWN

giant minds and heavy hands,
their privilege towering
from a saucer-scraper
sunlight Sky Pad
castle in the clouds—
the gods only laugh
when the gorgon roars,
rocking her reptilian head,
neck in chains,
medusan voice
a cauldron of protest,
the state's broken beast
no honied and spiced
tender meat, soft
as a white lily

their big eyes glimmer
when the ambrosia cools
like coffee, pools,
amber as oil, viscous
as the blood of saints—
those onyx orbs brim
sentiments, read depths,
murky as a magic mirror

their toxic logic glistens,
smacks—they will never,
never free her, back off,
come down and join
the only-human
communal table,

address the jettisoned—
tarnished lives
who dwell below,
down in the gully,
shiver in cold shadow,
backs against
monolithic nights,
megalomaniacal schemes
of relative time—
toil long and hard,
count the days,
clock each clanging hour

trickle down politics?
only crocodile tears
trickle down,
down
    in the gully—
    so
    low,
    so
    hard,
    and
    so
    cold

A WAVE SHIFTS . . .

a wave shifts . . .
your face becomes your back
time mirror*
flipping echoes
flipping stars

*Physicists confirm their existence in a recent article by Eric Ralls at earth.com.

TERRAFORMING MARS

orbital mirror
glinting with warmth
thickening atmosphere

exhaling oxygen
greening into life
engineered microbes

thawing icecaps
by pressurized enclosures
a man-made lake

homestead
in the crook of a child's arm
little alien doll

EPOCECLIPSE WORD FIND

transhumans
sabotage
time mirrors
quantum leap
deep space

```
p j y q x o j t n u s e p m t w o p v x q y m u a k m i
g t m a v o w g d l m h q p z a e g t i m e m i r r o r s
o e g l v w c u h o l a q p v b r d l j e z x n s e q h d a
r s d h a a q u a r i u s k m b d e b o p w g j d q m i b
g s l j g s z c o p h r y d e i g c w p l j s q u n c i r s o
o r w k o f e p m e i y x w p k d e e p s p a c e m g t
n y t r a n s h u m a n s w k i g t s k m a e q p o d n a
y r w m h d p u k t w q k l d s i y b r e o f e l i f s e g
j g t e s p o l g s p r v i q p l j g s m b t o u d z y n i e
h c n r u s i p m c q u a n t u m l e a p s m k u h s q p
y w a i o n h r d x r w a c p l u f v k f e c p p y r z b t
o k w r v s l o i y g r s l n f v a p u b r w k g d q o p n
i g r d v p l a q x b t r p j t b l a w q o g w p a k b w k
```

www.ingramcontent.com/pod-product-compliance
Lightning Source LLC
Chambersburg PA
CBHW061247040426
42444CB00010B/2287